How to Get Your Ex Back

The Definitive Step-By-Step Guide To Rebuilding A
Strong Relationship And Winning Back Your Ex

*(The Definitive Guide To Quickly Reuniting With Your Ex
And Maintaining Your Lover Forever)*

Dennis Laroche

TABLE OF CONTNET

Be Frank And Truthful. 1

How To Keep Your Connection Strong And Expand After Utilizing 12

Love And Friendship: The Distinctions Between A Friend And A Lover. 46

Should You Begin Your New Relationship From Scratch When Dating Your Ex-Girlfriend? 65

Is It Valuable To Save? 108

Introduction 140

Be Frank And Truthful.

If you want your ex-girlfriend back, you have to be open and honest with her about your feelings and your intentions. This means giving her an explanation of your desire for reconciliation and your willingness to make concessions.

It's also imperative that you be honest with her about the changes you've made. Don't try to hide who you really are or make things too easy. She will be able to detect whether you're serious, and she will be more likely to give you another chance if she feels that you're determined to change.

If I may, have a look at this illustration of being honest and forthright with your ex-girlfriend:

● Clearly convey your feelings. Express more than simply "I love you" or "I miss you." Tell her everything about how you feel about her and how much you want to be with her again.

Accept responsibility for your mistakes. Take ownership of your role in the breakup and offer your condolences. Don't attempt to blame everything on her.

● Be truthful with your adjustments. Share with her the steps you've taken to strengthen your weaknesses and become a better version of yourself.

● Tell the truth about your intentions. Avoid trying to control her or giving her false hope. Be honest with them about what you want and are willing to provide.

You must be open and truthful with your ex-girlfriend if you hope to get her back. It shows her that you take the partnership seriously and that you're prepared to put in a lot of effort to maintain it.

Examples to Follow

Here's an example of how to speak with your ex-girlfriend in an honest and open manner:

"I truly apologize for the faults I made in our relationship and I accept responsibility for them. I've been improving as a person lately because I've been working on myself a lot. I communicate better, handle money more responsibly, and show greater emotional openness. I still think the world of you, and I want to get back to you. Even if I know I have to, I'm willing to go above and beyond to earn back your trust."

Being open and truthful with your ex-girlfriend is not always simple, but in the end, it's worth it. If she sees that you're prepared to put in the effort and have a sincere desire to change, she's more likely to give you another chance.

Allow Her Enough Time to Decide

After you've been open and sincere with your ex-girlfriend, it's important to allow her time to decide if she wants to get back together. She needs time to think things over because it's a big decision for her.

Don't force her to make a decision right now. Don't send her a ton of SMS or calls. Instead, give her some time to think things out.

When she decides whether or not she wants to reunite with you, you'll know. In the interim, put yourself first and live your life to the fullest.

Consider the following:

Don't put any pressure on her. Don't send her a ton of SMS or calls. Give her some time to consider the circumstances.

Pay attention to yourself. You ought not to hold off on making decisions about your life until she does. Continue living your life, doing the things that bring you joy.

● Be patient. She may decide to take action in the future. If she doesn't make a decision right away, please don't give up.

If you're polite and patient with your ex, she's more inclined to give you another chance.

For example

Here's an example of how to give your ex-girlfriend time to consider your offer:

"I understand that you need some time to reflect about if getting back together is truly what you want. I appreciate your decision and am willing to wait. In the interim, I'm going to focus on taking care of myself and making the most out of my life. I hope you will contact me when you're ready."

Giving your ex-girlfriend time to process the situation is important since it shows that you value her opinion. It also gives her the time and room to consider the relationship and decide what she wants out of it.

Chapter 4: How and When to Reconnect with Your Former Partner

Even while it is advised that you wait two, three, or even a month, the decision of when to contact again ultimately rests with you. However, even if two weeks have gone and you still feel wobbly and unconfident, just to be safe, DO NOT get back in touch just yet.

What dangers await you if you reconnect before you're ready? If things had not gone according to plan, there might have been even greater devastation and mental breakdown. If, for example, you reconnect and find out your ex is seeing someone else, you can lose it if you are not emotionally stable. The worst-case scenario is that you might cry and say harsh things in front of your ex if you are unable to control your emotions. During the No Contact phase, you want to build up a level of confidence and assurance that will enable you to move on from the unimaginable in the unlikely event that it occurs.

Still, it is imperative that you move swiftly. One month should be the ideal amount of time without communication. Since your ex and you are still just getting to know one another, you probably have a chance to win them back, even if you find out after a month that they are seeing someone else. You have an advantage since you will know what makes your ex smile, as well as their likes and dislikes because you know them so well.

establishing communication

Resuming contact can take a lot of different shapes. Depending on how your ex is feeling, you may choose to handle things gently or to make a big deal out of it.

If you know that spending time with your ex-partner will make them feel better about themselves, and they are hopeless romantics who love surprises, you can pull off a very amazing move by suddenly, bluntly, and unexpectedly inviting them to a fancy dinner date. This is, of course, presuming that your ex isn't already seeing someone else. Just make sure it's very clear that this isn't a lure to get back together but rather an offer to have a great meal, chat, and reignite the relationship. You can reconnect, but hold off on discussing your romance just now. Spending time together and reliving your dating days are more important than anything else when using this method. If you have the confidence and sex to pull it off, this will be a fun way to reignite your love.

Alternatively, you could send a fast text or email, or you might go the traditional route and meet your ex in person when you happen to run into them in the hallway. If you and your kids are still living together, you can start a small conversation or ask about your work or the kids' education.

How you proceed is ultimately up to you, but before you do, be sure your emotions are under control. You don't want to start a conversation with your ex-partner only to have a quarrel break out. If you are confident that all difficulties have been settled, it is best to get back in touch.

The following signs suggest that your ex-partner might be keen to reconnect with you:

Your ex responds when you say hi.

The gift you give your ex is accepted.

The conversation flows naturally, and their voice comes across as non-aggressive.

Their body language is relaxed, and they are facing you.

They respond to questions with detailed responses.

How To Keep Your Connection Strong And Expand After Utilizing

"The Rule of No Contact"

Resurfacing doubts, anxiety, and hurt feelings is the worst thing that can happen to you after you and your ex have reconciled. It's critical to keep in mind the lesson the split taught us. Compromises ought to be outlined if anything needs to be altered or given up. You need to alter something about yourself in order for a relationship to survive a split. Only when this happens will you both feel like the past is behind you. Here's the key to ensuring that a partnership will go on after a breakup. It's similar to ignoring the problem that initially led to the breakup. Especially if you are the one who created the error, try to make a sacrifice.

Modify something reasonable, attainable, long-lasting, and sensible. What does this signify? This means that when you make a change, be careful. It's not something you briefly quit doing to please your ex just to pick up the habit again after the dust settles. Never make a long-term commitment to change something. Don't pledge to give up drinking, for instance. Seek assistance from peers, physicians, and counselors instead. This demonstrates to your partner your real desire to change.

To improve their relationship, some couples go to further lengths and make significant sacrifices. If their physical separation is the issue, then preparing to move in together is the solution. If past infidelity is the cause, all suspicions can be eliminated by being more forthcoming and honest regarding schedules, online account passwords, and mobile phone use. Some married couples apply for higher-paying employment or seek the advice of financial consultants if their inability to make ends meet is the issue. Some decide to start over and relocate their entire family to a different nation.

You should only make the huge move if you are certain it will ultimately be beneficial for the harmony in your relationship or your family. Some sacrifices can genuinely change someone's life. For love, what are you prepared to give up?

New Beginning

Couples might rekindle their interest in one another under the No Contact Rule.

This presents an opportunity to reignite the spark that existed between them in their early stages. Don't let up if you have applied for No Contact successfully. Your lover might be feeling differently about you by now. Plan a trip together or go on more date nights to keep the spark alive. Maintain your new routines, interests, and optimistic outlook on life. But never lose sight of the fact that your absence brought you together. Every now and again, give yourself enough room to breathe so that you can miss each other. Every now and then, eat dinner by yourself or with a close buddy. Go to your hometown or accomplish the goal you've had for a very long time.

Initially, relationships can need a lot of labor and emotional challenges. To create harmony, many concessions and sacrifices are necessary. However, not every marriage that lasted for decades experienced a happy life together. They experienced relationship issues as well. The only thing that has changed is that they have taken action to resolve the issue rather than giving up. Prepare to adhere to the No Contact Rule if you truly want your ex back.

Chapter 6: Creating a Stress-Free Reunion Environment

The best thing you can ever do for yourself in a relationship is this. By acknowledging your previous errors and embracing the possibility that you will have to make amends in the future, you can make the path straight and easy. Although there is never a simple relationship, we attempt to keep it lively by avoiding the easy mistakes that we are prone to make on a regular basis. Make an effort to celebrate with your partner and give yourself permission to be hidden and motivated by the love you shared in the past. It is time to remember the wonderful times you two had in the past. It's true that you can handle a reunion without worry now that you have a thorough understanding of the common reasons why relationships end.

How to Get Ready for a Smooth Reunion

A seamless, stress-free reunion can be achieved by following a straightforward process. Dealing with a breakup is never easy. It is hard to be composed when you lose someone you love. But you have to keep yourself cool; it's a guaranteed method to win your ex back. Some of these are common blunders made by persons who are attempting to win their ex back. If you want your ex back in your arms, try to steer clear of the following negative situations as much as you can.

Transform yourself

Recall that getting your ex back is not an easy feat. The situation will only get worse if you start acting strangely and make promises to yourself that you'll change in order to get your girlfriend back. Right now, everything you do should be sincere and truthful. Avoid appearing hopeless and unable to regulate your emotions. It doesn't seem like your ex decided to part ways with you based on your personal traits or characteristics. Should that be the case, they wouldn't have waited until now to end their relationship. You can, however, alter certain aspects of yourself without going too far.

very attentive to other people

This is a typical error made by those attempting to reunite with their former partner. You're likely to receive advice from people everywhere after telling your friends and family. It appears that everyone has an opinion on the subject that they believe to be correct. You need to use caution while selecting advisors. Remember, you know your former partner better than anyone else. This important reminder will, therefore, enable you to quickly sort through all of the positive and negative remarks.

Continue working to get them back.

Are you really interested in regaining your ex? You have to do your hardest! This entails carefully considering your options, making a plan, and then acting! Even when they know deep down that they truly want their ex-partner back, some people purposefully put off thinking about getting them back. They believe they may enjoy a little time together as a single before reuniting as a couple. Therefore, this is a massive no-no. Remember that your ex can decide to leave you permanently; therefore, extending the time would only allow them to distance themselves from you.

conversing via a third party

After the breakup, all you do and say counts; being outspoken makes it difficult to stay composed. However, saying anything amusing could just lead to more distance between the two of you. Asking a third party to deliver a message is a common mistake made by many people. Give up! Never presume that someone else can do the task for you. Inform your former partner personally. Additionally, when spoken by someone else, the messages may alter, which could result in more errors.

If you take the time to carefully consider each step and create a plan for what you want to achieve in the end, you may avoid a lot of post-breakup problems. Make an effort to regulate your feelings, and proceed with extreme caution when taking advice from others. You don't want to commit any more errors. Thus, exercise greater caution, have faith in your judgment, and steer clear of blunders to ensure a happy reconciliation.

Chapter 8: Is less really more? The mystery of absence

Is the proverb" absence makes the heart grow fonder" something you've heard before? If so, you might be asking how this old knowledge could be relevant to your circumstances. Maybe you're wondering if it's possible to move on from your ex and if letting quiet grow between the two of you might lead to a reconciliation. You question, is less really more?

I am here to inform you that it is possible to have more with less. However, I also want you to understand that being absent is not a deceptive tactic. It's not about vanishing to hope your ex would miss you and come back to you. No, absence may be a very effective instrument for personal growth and self-discovery if handled appropriately. Absence ultimately speaks more about you than it does about your ex.

Do you recall our discussion of the significance of introspection for self-discovery in Chapter 3? And when did we talk about the significance of personal regeneration in Chapter 6? These concepts are closely related to absence, which gives you the time and space to concentrate on yourself, heal, and develop personally.

We must first comprehend why absence is effective before we can appreciate its actual enchantment. Have you ever yearned for something that is out of your reach? Have you ever noticed that something seems to become more appealing when it is harder to get? This is the core of human desire psychology.

Think about how rarity affects how we value things. We place a higher value on items that are uncommon or challenging to obtain. This idea underpins the diamond economy, the allure of limited editions, and the demand for premium memberships. More important than the item itself is the excitement of possessing something rare or out of reach. Recall from Chapter 2 that we discussed the stages of grieving and how losing a loved one might make us feel more intensely for them. The same idea is used in the absence but in a healthier and more beneficial way.

However, this does not imply that you should isolate yourself or turn into an unapproachable monolith. Not at all. Rather, it implies that you have to acquire the skill of being less reachable and accessible. It entails giving oneself space to breathe, live your life, and pursue your own passions and interests. It entails establishing sound limits and having the ability to say "n" when called for.

Naturally, there's a thin line here between being less approachable and aloof or indifferent. Avoid going too far in the other direction and ultimately pushing your ex away. However, generally speaking, intrigue and curiosity can be piqued by a little mystery and unreachability.

Take time to consider this: isn't it what draws us into a great book, a captivating film, or even a mystery stranger? It's the sensation that you are never fully informed and that there is always more to learn. The quiet in a song, the break in a discussion, or the empty space on a canvas are what draw our attention and arouse feelings of longing and yearning. I'll tell you what, though: if you handle your absence properly, it can be the quiet, stop, or blank space that draws people in.

I want to use a remark from Dr. Esther Perel, a well-known relationship psychologist, from her book "Mating in

Captivity" (2006). She contends that a long-term relationship needs a balance between security and surprise in order to sustain desire. While we require a sense of security and belonging, we also require room to be free and self-sufficient. We must be able to shift between dependence and independence, between proximity and distance. Even if you are not in a relationship with your ex, the same principle still holds true in this situation.

Aside from fostering your independence and self-awareness, being absent can help you see your previous relationship from a fresh angle. Often, it is challenging to view things objectively when we are fully engaged in a situation.

As they say, "You can't see the forest for the trees," but if you take a step back and give yourself permission to be away from that circumstance, you can start to see things from a wider perspective. It will be possible for you to observe the dynamics, patterns, and successful and unsuccessful strategies. Gaining knowledge from prior experiences is crucial for personal development.

Renowned author Mark Manson discusses how suffering can be essential to our development as individuals. Even though it can hurt at first, being absent can be one of those experiences that helps you grow in knowledge and self-awareness over time.

Lastly, I want you to picture yourself as an artistic creation. Have you ever noticed that the best paintings are positioned so that there is adequate room around them to really appreciate them? How come the most beautiful sculptures are displayed separately from the others on a pedestal? The artwork can be fully appreciated in its splendor because of this area and the lack of outside distractions. Likewise, your absence might make it easier for your ex to recognize your worth.

Naturally, none of this ensures that your former partner will quickly reconcile with you. That's alright, too. Ultimately, being absent is more about rediscovering who you are than it is about getting your ex back. Doesn't that seem like an exciting prospect?

It is nothing new that the power of absence may be seen in many facets of life. Allow me to transport you back in time to 1926 when Ludwig van Beethoven—one of the greatest musical geniuses ever—wrote a letter to his enduring sweetheart. Beethoven, who was incredibly in love, spent a lot of time apart from his sweetheart, and it was at that time that his emotions became stronger and his love became more profound. In it, he uttered the words, "My angel, my all, my self." They both got the chance to want and yearn for one another throughout that time of absence.

Is it not evident how this idea has accompanied us throughout history?

#5: DO NOT PERUSE THEM

Make it your new routine to just not read his texts if you know that your phones are configured so that he will see them when you do so. This will be really challenging because, if he DOES text you from time to time, you'll be wondering if there's a note of apology or "I love you" in there. It will still be there when you're ready to get in touch with him, so don't worry. This also applies to Facebook communications, which we will discuss in a moment.

#6: OH, and FACEBOOK,

Yes, this is quite the beast! Whether a relationship is going on or not, Facebook is a great tool. After a breakup, there's a thin line between good and evil. In the end, you can always tell when they are online, which is unhealthy for you both. If all goes according to plan, he will eventually start checking to see when you're online and if you do your part and don't bug him. He will merely block you if you bother him, and that hurts more than anything else. It doesn't matter when he is online, so don't even bother checking it. Remove him from your list of friends.

#7: DO NOT USE FACEBOOK MESSAGE

This is really crucial! For any reason, avoid sending him a Facebook message. It's not necessary to remove your previous communications because, occasionally, they're rather charming to peruse. Don't message him here, though; it's the same as sending a text, and some ladies handle things differently on social media. Ladies, I'm here to inform you that it's the same thing! Don't do it.

#8: VALUE HIS SOCIAL MEDIA SPACE AND TIME

Social media provides users with an outlet after a demanding day and allows them to do whatever they choose. He doesn't need you to continually tell him that you are there; it's kind of like when you watch TV or hang out with the guys. This would be similar to knowing that his friend will be at his place every evening after work. It does not necessarily mean that he wants to talk to you just because you can see that he is online. Just as you would want your mother or grandmother to respect your privacy, you should also respect his online time. Better yet, disregard his presence entirely on the internet.

#9: CONTINUE TO BE YOURSELF. Don't alter your online behaviors in any way. Continue posting what you have for breakfast if you do so every morning. You should spend your days eating Cheetos on your shirt and lounging around your house surrounded by twenty cats. You take care of yourself better than ever, exactly as you always do.

#10-(In a similar vein) AVOID TRYING TO BE SOMEONE ELSE

In the same way, avoid attempting to be someone you're not or even another version of yourself. Trying to suddenly become a gym rat or health fanatic won't make him fall in love with you this time either, as he didn't fall for that version of you the prior time. Do it! If you frequently share a photo of yourself with your favorite pizza and cozy socks while football is on TV in the background, then go ahead and do it! Never try to act or be someone you're not to win him back. Your friends will notice it, to start with, and some of them may even call you out on it! They might be wondering why you're not crocheting like you usually do but rather spending all your time rock climbing. Furthermore, you don't want to have to blame the split for the changes in your life. It's best just to keep being who you are and plugging away. However, if you have taken up rock climbing because it is something you have always wanted to attempt, then go for it! Just make sure you are being sincere.

#11: CARE FOR YOURSELF

Need a pedicure? Go for it. Do you want to get a new hair color? Go big! And go ahead and upload a photo of it on the internet (take one for yourself). You should be proud to flaunt your new haircut or manicure as you received them for YOU and no one else. You deserve to see that movie and have that Starbucks cup, so go ahead and do it!

#12-AVOID OVERDOSING IT

Steer clear of sharing photos of yourself partying and getting inebriated at the club on Facebook, Twitter, or Snapchat when your face is covered in club makeup. Don't do it now either if you're not the kind to wear a lot of makeup, aren't a party animal, and don't normally drink. He will see right through your desperate attempts to make him envious in order to show him what he is lacking. It's a major turnoff. You don't want to be inebriated when making phone calls, girl; therefore, alcohol isn't your greatest buddy right now (a slap on the wrist).

He is, in fact, missing out. But you simply keep rocking YOU, so it won't last long.

If you are plagued by constant worry, anxiety, and compulsive thoughts about your breakup, you are more likely to make mistakes that aggravate your ex and heighten your anxiety.

As an example,

You might suppose that if your ex calls, they want to make amends and start feeling your love for them again.

You could be tempted to drive to your ex's house with gifts of chocolate and flowers if they tell you they still have feelings for you, as you think this is the kind of happy ending you see in movies.

If your ex and someone of the other sex post a picture together on social media, you might believe they're dating and start worrying and making all the mistakes I just said.

If you find out that someone likes a photo on Instagram, you might automatically assume that they want to go to bed with them. You may become irrational or almost insane, lose it, and give them a call.

The strongest defense against misinterpretations is to just stop acting for a while. Not until your mind is no longer frantically panicked and has calmed down. It's also a good idea to ignore your loved ones' advice at this time. Most people, even with the best of intentions, are ill-equipped to evaluate a breakup and decide how to proceed in order to get their love back.

What happens if I've made mistakes in the past?

After the breakup, you've most likely already made at least one of these mistakes. Fear not; after a divorce, even Harvard psychologists and the wisest monks in the Himalayas often make the same mistakes.

It is in human nature to try to cling to objects that have special importance to them. Reward yourself not for it.

The most important thing you can do now is realize that you can't win him back with these mistakes and stop making them immediately. Proceed to the next step of the strategy, which is to undo all the damage you've previously caused.

What will they think if I don't communicate with my former partner for thirty or sixty days? It's a legitimate question.

Actually, that's not a very good question. It's a question that your overworked mind will undoubtedly ask.

We can never know what is going through someone else's mind, as I have said before. Not unless we are capable of telepathy.

But I can tell you what usually happens to an ex after they stop talking to them after a breakup.

After your breakup, if you and your ex maintained contact, they never really had to handle it. Yes, they made the decision to break up with you, and they probably thought it was the right one.

But they never had to deal with the split since you kept acting as though you were still with them.

You lose someone you love when you break up. And if they never actually experienced the breakup, if they never felt like they lost you.

They never cried; they never felt like there was a black hole from hell in the pit of their stomachs. There's a good chance your ex may begin to feel wounded when you break up. How people deal with that sadness is a whole other conversation;

They may begin contacting you on a regular basis.

They could get angry.

They may completely cease replying to you. Don't panic; this is usually just a temporary scenario. Tell your worried thoughts to calm down.

Through mutual contacts or on social media, they might start following you.

They might even decide to keep quiet about their split until they have moved on.

They may want to get in touch with you on the side to see how you're doing and to act as though they're considering you. Put another way, they'll give you a bone. And if you accept it, they'll see that you're still their pet and totally in charge.

Love And Friendship: The Distinctions Between A Friend And A Lover.

Are you a little confused about why your friend has been acting so strangely over the past few weeks? What's causing you to pay so much attention?

Do you think he would fall in love with you? You may be thinking correctly about how he behaves while you are around.

Friendship and love are two distinct concepts that are frequently misunderstood by some. If there are still questions and you're unsure about anything, you should think about these. Herearesomeofthemostnoticeablesigns that canclassifyloveandfriendship.

1. A Lover Forgets; A Friend Forgives

A true friend is someone who will always be willing to forgive you, regardless of how big your mistakes are. Yes, they will forgive you, but never forget what you have done. Somehow, you'll get their trust back, but the thing is, they won't ever forget anything.

A lover is someone who, regardless of everything you've done, will still be able to forgive all of your mistakes and feel as though nothing has ever happened.

2. A friend who always stays. Be the next person you meet; a lover will do

everything just to be with you. Love and friendship can sometimes have the same meaning. A friend is always there when you need someone to talk to. When you need one, they will lend a helping hand. You may be yourself, share your secrets with them, and let your heart show. However, if a lover is there, it could be difficult for him to just look into your eyes. A lover is willing to sacrifice a lot of things every day to be with you.

3. A Friend Is Willing to Wait Long Hours; A lover will Wait Until Nevertheless, your friends will wait for you, but eventually, they will become weary and decide not to stay. Throughout the several hours of watching, you will undoubtedly hear all

the clarifications. A lover will patiently wait for you till you arrive and hear nothing but pure worries. Both love and friendship are deemed to be individually unique. It only requires a thorough examination of the subject's actions, particularly about you.

4. A friend will laugh at you if you do anything careless and foolish; a lover will become angry if these things occur.

When you've done something that undoubtedly upsets you, and you feel like you've wounded yourself a little, your friends are the ones who should be there first. Not to validate you but to laugh at your flaws.

A lover will be enthralled with you and will even nag you for your stubbornness.

Why? The reason it's not so obvious is that she cares.

5. A Friend's Thoughts About Today; A Lover's Thoughts About The Future

Different perspectives must be taken on friendship and love. Friends are always there during evenings and weekends, so at some point, they will be thinking about what you two will be doing together for the remainder of the day.

A lover thinks of a future with you, too, not just for today or tomorrow, but a future with a happy family, not just the two of you.

Unmistakable Indications That a Man Is in Love with You - What Every Woman Must Have Known

We are all in awe at times, regardless of whether the man we are with is falling deeply in love with us or with him.

In case you are with a woman right now, and you are unsure if her heart belongs to you or not, and she is simply silent about her feelings, assistance might be provided.

Here are some ways to find out what he's thinking based only on paying close attention to his activities. It is not necessary for you to sit and wonder if he truly loves you or not.

1. Raises the "manlily" things to be One of the several indications that a man is in love with you is when he gives you "ordinary" things or things he simply loves to be with.

For instance, he might extend an invitation to visit the bar with the guys or offer to buy you a night of beer just to spend some time with them. Should he have a passion for flying, you might discover him taking a week off work to join you on a date.

You can betray a lot of faith in him, and he'll probably be called "whipped" by his buddhĖes for this. Therefore, you may feel confident that you have a special place in his heart if he presents you with these kinds of opportunities to be with him.

2- WHAT SHE REALLY SEEES You know things about yourself that others don't (maybe even he sees things you don't!) He describes your interactions with others, how people perceive you in public, how your mind functions, how you handle emotions, and how you express yourself.

He pays attention to all the small details and remembers them. He accepts you for the whole package—the good and the bad.

Not only does she love you, but she also loves things about you. Truly loving someone doesn't mean that you love them for who they are (despite the belief held by many that this is the definition of love). Rather, it's about accepting them for who they are. This kind of love is unrelated to how good a person makes you feel about yourself.

Not that someone you love can't or won't make you feel good about yourself, but you can't really love someone just because they make you feel good.

That is a very different kind of love—one that satisfies your need to feel good right then and there rather than a deep, life-altering kind.

When someone truly sees you, they see not just what you are but also what you want to be, and they will let you know when you are falling short. Thecatch? This could actually make you feel self-conscious.

Somebody who loves you will let you know if you're acting rudely toward strangers, treating friends poorly, or failing to live up to your obligations. Even though it doesn't seem right, it's a sign that he truly sees you and cares about you.

3. Identifying Ways To Enhance You realize that a man is in love with you when he tries to find ways to impress you. Every woman has a different approach to improving her privileges. For example, he might send you flowers or leave you without a card.

He might spend the next few days fixing your car for you. He might cook you a nice dinner and have a romantic evening with you. Whatever the situation, if he is making an effort to try and impress you, then you are unquestionably more than "just another girl" in his eyes.

Take a Break

Your heart is hurting since you recently split up. All you want to do is return there and demonstrate to them that everything was only misunderstood. Believe me when I say this. Remain absent.

Am I telling the truth? Yes, I am, I assure you. Don't be angry with your ex; instead, allow them room to breathe. They do not want to see you right now, and frequent visits just make them angry, so avoid them.

The following is what I mean when I say "stay away":

Avoid calling them just to say hello. Avoid tweeting or sending them instant messages.

Avoid texting

Not a single amusing status update on the internet

No "bumping" them because you were in the same neighborhood. No getting together with pals.

Just keep your distance and leave it at that. You two require some distance.

This is known as the "no contact rule," which you should strictly adhere to if you truly want your ex back.

I love my ex, so why can't I give myself a break?

Yes, I am aware of how deeply you feel, but we are not just focusing on your emotions at this time—we are also considering those of your former partner. You must take a moment to consider everything.

It's not the finest idea, despite what you may believe, to go back to them. Why are you going back to the gun even if you need to put a bandage on your wound when you are not sober because your heart was just hurt?

Alright, let's tend to the wound first. That's the reason.

You're wondering why your ex is leaving you, and your head is cluttered. You must leave in order to clear your head.

Going back right away indicates that you do not want to be aware of the errors you committed that might have added to the circumstance.

No one consistently consumes the same kind of food. Allow your ex to feel your absence. They grow weary of you since they see you all the time.

If you're serious about getting someone back, you should consider these three points.

Yes, I am aware that you are wondering what you are expected to do in this silent moment. Alright, let's investigate.

How Should I Use My Time Off?

You are most likely to make mistakes while you are taking time off. This is because, even though it's a break for you and your ex, you should be spending time improving yourself. While it's acceptable for you to mourn the end of the relationship, you must get up and begin the process of healing if you hope to rekindle that love.

Let's examine a few options for you to consider during this time.

Modifying your look

You no longer look like the old you. Look, you've changed into a whole new species! Take action to improve your image. You'll feel good about yourself, your self-esteem will soar, and your ex will be astounded if they see you, I promise.

You can obtain a good short haircut if your hair is long. To acquire that amazing smile, visit the dentist and get your teeth whitened.

You ought to visit the gym to tone your muscles and drop a few pounds. Finally, you may switch up your clothes.

Now is not the time to spend long evenings in bars consuming copious amounts of ice cream or alcohol until dawn. Now is the ideal moment to reinvent yourself.

Adjust your perspective.

You should take action to change your attitude toward your ex and life in general because your attitude affects your altitude. Accept thankfulness in everything. Appreciate the positive and negative experiences you shared with your former partner.

Have self-confidence and happiness. You are totally responsible for making yourself happy, so go about it and have fun. Take travels, visit the beach, and spend time with your folks. Look for ways to bring joy to your heart.

Maintain a notebook.

Keep a journal of your daily encounters. You will not realize that you are going through a process until it is over. Put in writing what you discovered or what you found difficult. Keep this journal well because when you get back with your ex, you will read it together. You can also let all of your emotions out by keeping a journal.

Pray

It's time to embark on a spiritual journey during this moment when you feel isolated. Think about everything. You'll have a deeper understanding of your own strengths and shortcomings. Above all, you'll be able to love and accept yourself for who you are. This is what will develop confidence since there are no doubts holding you back. You are aware of this.

Discover something new

Are you able to bake or cook? Are you an accomplished painter or musician? Look, there were some things you were unable to accomplish the last time you were with your ex. What reason is there to not acquire fresh knowledge? This isn't just about passing the time; it's also about developing new abilities and self-reinvention.

Make new acquaintances.

Why not meet new friends and enjoy yourself with them since you don't want to become too attached to your ex?

You've completed the time steps and are now sober enough to examine your connection with your former partner.

Should You Begin Your New Relationship From Scratch When Dating Your Ex-Girlfriend?

Alright, your efforts have worked off because you and your ex-girlfriend are again together. What, then, must you do at this point? When you are dating your ex-girlfriend again, should you start your new relationship from the beginning? Or should you just keep dating her in the same manner as before? As if nothing had occurred? Well, perhaps it's not quite that easy.

The only goal of this post is to examine whether it's necessary to begin your new relationship with your ex-girlfriend from scratch. Keep in mind that everything ultimately depends on you and that this is merely a guideline.

Here are some places to start if you need to rebuild your relationship from the beginning.

Do you still act irrationally? You have likely evolved over time to make your characters more suited to one another. Therefore, it is crucial that you are able to remain composed in any situation. This is due to the possibility that she will choose to put you to the test to determine if you are the new guy you say you are. As you can see, it is now recommended that you truly start from scratch.

Do you schedule the majority of your dates in advance? It really shouldn't be an issue to plan ahead if you've dated her multiple times. Any other man in your position would struggle to find ways to win her over with things that she finds appealing. To you, the next date ought to practically always arrange itself.

You don't ponder where to take her all the time. That's because, during the course of your previous relationship, she undoubtedly stated a number of destinations she wished to see you. You will, therefore, have another opportunity to start your relationship with the love of your life by going out with her again, and this time, it will be perfect.

Getting her to laugh is simpler. This is because you are aware of all of her behaviors, preferences, and likes. No matter how funny your jokes are, you should have perfected the art of making your girl laugh by now. And the reason for that is that the way you say something to her will make her laugh more than what you say.

You already are the perfect suitor. Why would you ask? It is, in fact, incredibly easy. You used to be her suitor, but you broke up with her because you two weren't ideal. Because you want to give yourself another chance at love, you have both eventually changed for the better. Thus, rather than starting from scratch, you should build on what you already have.

What is the conclusion, then? Is it necessary to start over when dating your ex-girlfriend? The solution lies between in the middle; for the most part, you only need to build on what you've already had with her, but for smaller issues like changing your character, you need to start over from scratch.

Chapter 7: Is It Truly A First Date When You Go Out With Your Ex-Girlfriend?

Alright, so your perseverance has paid off, and you and your ex-girlfriend are once again together. What comes next, then? As you may have observed, the memorable first date moment recurs in every aspect of your life. But when you are dating your ex, does that truly qualify as your first date? Or perhaps you ought to view it as a second opportunity? Actually, everything depends.

This article's only goal is to provide you with a satisfactory response to the question of whether or not the first date you went on with your ex-girlfriend was actually your first.

You should think about a few starting points in order to effectively respond to that question.

1. To what extent are you anxious? You can judge for yourself how apprehensive you get by remembering back to the classic first date. You really do take it as a first date if it makes you feel anxious for no apparent reason. You may have a point; getting too close to the girl of your

dreams is never possible. Nevertheless, when you are going out with someone you have known for a long time, nervousness shouldn't normally play a role. From that perspective, it shouldn't be seen as a first date because it won't be with a total stranger.

2. What should you say to her, exactly? Is a straightforward response even necessary for this one? You pretty much already know all of her favorite topics of conversation. When it comes to stammering at her and eventually bringing her to the point of ending the date, you have an absolute advantage over any other man who could have been in your position.

3. You are aware of the ideal location. Knowing the location where you two feel completely at ease with one another gives you an additional advantage when it comes to setting up a first date with your ex. Therefore, if you had to predict where she intended to go, you could have once again labeled it a first date.

4. You're skilled at making her chuckle. Make a girl giggle, and she will truly start to appreciate your company. If you were dating someone else, this endeavor would be extremely challenging; however, when your ex-girlfriend is involved, it becomes less challenging. You are in complete control of the situation.

5. You possess the attributes she seeks in an ideal man. Well, you may not be flawless, but in her eyes, you are flawless.

6. You are aware of what to get her. You would have spent a long time debating whether or not to bring her something if this had been a true first date. As you are already aware of her preferences, this obviously cannot be the case in this instance.

Therefore, dating your ex-girlfriend can hardly be considered a first date, as you can choose for yourself. Since you two have known each other for a very long time, you don't feel any more pressure when you go out with her because she has grown to like you. Nothing about your date makes it particularly noteworthy to be the first.

Section Six

Show that you've changed, don't just say it.

One of the hardest things you will ever go through in life is a breakup.

You'll experience unbearable pain that feels like it's physicalizing your emotional anguish.

It will feel as though the world is collapsing around your crushed heart. Everybody has, at some point in their lives, gone through something similar. Although time heals all wounds, grief invariably leaves some sort of lifetime scar.

❖ Belief

Belief relationships terminate for a reason; that can't happen because there's a lack of love and no happiness. Something isn't operating properly.

There are endless disputes, falsified information, persistent pestering, lying, and a lack of respect.

Both partners' physical and emotional needs must be satisfied for the partnership to succeed. If not, then everything breaks down from that point on.

However, if you were the one in a relationship that ended, how would you respond?

And what if you were completely blind to it?

Say you still have feelings for your ex-partner.

What if your behaviors caused him/her to become dissatisfied in the relationship, and you were unaware of it?

What happens if I keep going?

What happens if your only wish for him/her is to return your love?

There are many possibilities.

It's critical to first consider what went wrong if you want to reconcile with your ex.

Admitting that your actions caused the relationship to end might be challenging.

The next step is to own up to your mistakes and extend your apology.

You have to face your own beast before you can count on your ex to return.

Have you ever cheated or lied while you were dating?

Was it violent?

Did you fail to treat them with the decency they merit?

Will you do all it takes to keep your relationship intact?

Saying "I apologize" is far too simple.

Yes, you mean business, but asking for forgiveness is more crucial.

It is one thing to apologize; it is another to demonstrate it.

Showing your former partner that you've evolved is fantastic, but you must first convince yourself of this. If you are sincere, your ex-boyfriend will be able to tell.

Consider the reasons behind your previous negative behavior that led to the end of a relationship.

Why did I mislead, steal, or mistreat?

Once you have the answer, work on yourself.

If you're not pleased with yourself, it's impossible to be entirely happy in your relationships.

You can ask your ex-lover to give you another chance with confidence once you have resolved your own problems.

Prove to him/her that you are not going to continue doing the things that led to the breakup.

- Distressing Divorce

The hardest separations are unpleasant ones. They can appear to need a significant amount of time to identify the problems and live, and occasionally, they have no success rate at all.

When something outrageous happens, there are unpleasant separations. Perhaps your ex made fun of you or fell hard for someone else. If your former partner was violent and zealous, that will also cause a deep emotional distance.

Here's the question: Despite all of the terrible things your ex has done to you, are you willing to swear off using makeup and everything else with them? Can you continue living a happy life in this manner?

The question here isn't going to be how long it will take your ex to come back, but rather, how long it will take for you both to move on and stop looking back.

This is the same reason we advise a no-contact period of roughly one month to allow you to gather your thoughts. Severe separations might cause conflict. To understand what went wrong in your relationship and how to put things right, you need to discover contentment in yourself and the situation.

If you truly believe that you love your ex and that you must let go of all the painful memories, then go ahead and tell them.

In the unlikely event that your former partner believes they can handle this relationship, you may be able to quickly resolve issues. Just make sure that the cruelty of the past doesn't carry over into your current partnership.

Obtaining your ex back may take five to ten months due to extreme separations. However, there's a danger that, in the event that your ex never really makes the relationship work, you'll never be able to win them back. If your relationship is once again at a standstill and your former partner isn't showing any signs of improvement, it's best to give up and move on.

Section Five

FIGHTS FOR REUNITING AS ONE

If you believe that getting back together with your ex is the best option, think about your next course of action.

Although there will undoubtedly be many challenges to overcome, being reunited does not guarantee that you will live happily ever after.

This is especially clear if your split hasn't gone as planned and there have been a lot of hurtful remarks and mudslinging exchanged between the two of you.

When deciding whether getting back together would be the best course of action, keep the following in mind:

• Press the rewind button.

It's normal to miss your ex and want to get back together with someone you once loved, but is it wise for you to do so?

There were probably a lot of heated deals throughout the time you were both competing and splitting apart. And there may have been angry, agonizing words exchanged between the two parties.

In any event, you two might be able to carry on even together with a little effort, sincerity, and forgiveness on both ends.

Opening the secret compartment

So, after telling the world how much you hated your ex and thought the worst of everything about them, how can you reveal that you've gotten back together? This may seem a little strange to you because you may believe that the people closest to you deserve an explanation. What's the best course of action for you? Just speak the truth.

- Changing the way your parents think

There's also the problem of trying to change your parents' opinions about your former partner.

When you eventually split up, you most likely told them all the "dreadful" things your ex had done when you got home, crying and upset. Maybe, just maybe, you exaggerated your account to present your then-accomplice in a negative light.

How might you convince them to like your ex again now that you two are back together? Most likely, they'll tell you to just go get someone else.

• Bets made at a distance

After all the drama and tears, friends will support your decision to get back together with your former partner. Additionally, there will also be some people who will undoubtedly think you're crazy.

You run the danger of losing your friends' trust since they won't support your decisions in the future.

Additionally, they might make fun of your struggles the next time you talk to them about problems involving your former partner.

• Virtual amusement complain

Of course, there's the matter of re-engaging with one another through online entertainment again. Despite your best efforts, people will notice this and start talking because nothing is private anymore.

In the unlikely event that that is not all, you will need to update your relationship status again, and friends who are keeping an eye out for your notices won't overlook this.

Leap for unpredictability

Your partnership will never be the same after all the hardship and heartache caused by your split. You can both inquire about your true mental processes in a cooperative manner.

Studies reveal that those who have been separated from and reunited with their former partner are more prone to uncertainty. Sadly, that tiny, unsettling bundle of doubt will always remain in the pit of your stomach.

You may be overjoyed for the first few days or weeks of your reunion, but there's a chance that you'll hear a voice in the back of your mind asking, "How long is this going to last this time?" Will you have to travel with someone you don't totally trust?

- Is this a different romantic relationship?

Even while it's easy to decide to hold onto it and let it bother you, getting back together means that you both have to make a conscious *and extra hard* effort to start over.

Is it similar to another partnership? That's something you both need to resolve. That being said, there is no question about it: if you continue to be the same and don't make any progress, your relationship will end tragically soon.

Chapter 3: Ask Yourself If You Really Want Your Ex Back

Of the three important questions posed at the start of this book, which do you still remember asking yourself? Do you still have feelings for your ex? You probably think you can skip this chapter if you answer "yes" to that question. However, rationally, it might not be the case at all.

Relationships are one of the many gray areas in life, but there are still good and terrible reasons to want your ex back.

A Moment To Ponder

Certain connections are destined to endure forever and become stronger over time. But some relationships are better left in the past and forgotten, or they are doomed from the beginning. This chapter will teach you whether your reasons for wanting to reconcile with your ex-partner will work in your favor or against you.

You're Still Attached To Your Ex

This is perhaps the best argument in favor of attempting to get your ex back. Actually, the outcome is merely coincidental. For now, the only thing that counts is that you tried your hardest. If everything doesn't work out in the end, at least you won't spend your life worrying about what more you could have done to win your ex back.

You are accountable for the past events that occurred.

Even while love and guilt can both be strong emotions, using guilt as a reason to get your ex back is not a good idea. You just have to learn to live with your guilt until time and forgiveness allow it to disappear if there is no love. Reuniting with an ex-lover out of remorse can only cause further suffering.

You'd Really Like to Give It Another Go

While that might not be the best argument to get your ex back, it's also not a bad one. You can still fall in love even though it's likely that none of you or either side fell in love with the other the first time.

If this is the reason you wish to make amends with your former partner, take care not to convey any false impressions about your plans. Lying is never a good foundation for a relationship, and it can also merely muddy the waters between you and your ex.

You believe that the Present is your fault.

You didn't end things badly when you broke up. But you started feeling bad when you found out how miserable your ex is right now. That makes logic, but it is not a compelling enough argument to reconcile with your ex. To find out if what you truly want to offer is an apology, companionship, or a second shot at love, you need to ask additional questions.

You sense isolation

It's undoubtedly one of the worst, if not the worst, justifications for wanting your ex back. Seeking solace from loneliness in your ex's company would be self-serving. You might benefit from getting back together with your ex, but what about them? Do you think it will impact your ex's feelings?

What will happen if the other person finds out why you really want to make amends? Is it going to be nice or bad?

You may have many reasons for this, not all of which are valid. In the end, you have to listen to your heart as much as your logic.

Is it really the correct thing to do, and is it something you really want back?

Put no emphasis on the result!

As delineated in Step 4: Discover your inner guy, men are risk-takers and daring to venture into unfamiliar territory.

This holds true for both ordinary life and dire circumstances. Particularly when you're interacting with other women, it's a risk you want to take in case she rejects you. You are not obsessed with her, and you don't base your sense of worth on what other people think of you. You won't display anxiety or nervousness about the result if you are straightforward and courteous to get right to the subject. Here, living fully in the moment is the key. You don't want your mind to go into hypothetical scenarios or negative outcomes for yourself. That is a time and energy waste. You should act how you are feeling right now and live in the Present.

This implies that you should never consider the future while interacting with a stunning girl. Ignore thoughts of how nice it would be to undress her or whether she would give you her number. You will naturally become more engaged in her than she has in you as a result of this uncomfortable situation.

As we've just said, allow her time to win you over. She must understand that it will take some work to get past your filter and that she will be proud of herself if she succeeds. Turn the narrative on its head and begin to perceive yourself as the winner.

Never pay attention to those pick-up artists that prey on women. It is unrelated to this at all. However, it's all about you discovering your inner man and projecting a confident, secure demeanor.

Keep an open mind about the result; she might surprise you.

I never even considered obtaining her phone number. Speaking with women who physically appeal to you is a terrific method to practice this. You want to show them how much you appreciate them, yet you'll soon turn around and go.

This will make a lasting impression on your mind and restore your confidence.

Let go. Avoid overthinking and overcomplicating issues.

Say hello to strangers first, please. Consider this: if you don't have the courage to follow through, would you rather have someone think ill of you or have to think poorly of yourself?

But don't be that dumbass who becomes completely hooked on a female in the hopes that he might score, adhering to her like glue. Be lively and enjoyable to be around. Speak with the girls and then release them.

Keep in mind that meeting new people—especially women—will greatly aid in your efforts to win your ex back, even if you don't feel like doing so! Women are aware of how they perform in relationships with other women. Men want to be like you, and women want to be with you when you're a successful man with other women. Though most women would have you believe otherwise, envy is actually a form of admiration and interest that is veiled. The feedback you receive from other women is crucial because, when it comes to males, they are all fierce competitors.

Imagine the following situation: you and your pals head to a club. Everything is going well; you act confident among the women, give sincere comments, flirt, and get away before they really get a good look. Being both rare and fascinating at the same time. Coincidentally, your ex's friend was present and witnessed everything.

You can be sure that by morning, your ex will be aware of this. Soon, you might hear about it.

However, you must attempt to embody this process rather than forcing it; once more, fake it until you create it. This goes way beyond simply giving your partner another chance.

This is a lesson you should teach all the girls in your life—they should never have enough of you. Make them enamored with you, and as soon as they begin to show interest, pounce back at the same speed that she is. Keep in mind the adage, "Two steps forward, one step back, yet still progressing."

It takes practice to get good at this. For a few weeks, I set a goal for myself to obtain a phone number every day! Women will make things very easy for you as you improve, and some may even offer you their number. I know you shouldn't be outcome-driven.

This is particularly effective if you go about and run into a woman you've spoken to before without getting her number. By then, you'll have shown her that you're not a helpless beta male and that you can manage a lady like her, which puts you in a very advantageous situation.

One thing to keep in mind is that the initial sexual tension will ultimately subside. If you don't make progress and insist on a gradual escalation of the issue, you'll find yourself trapped in the buddy zone. This implies that you should approach a female for a date at least the third time you see her. As your confidence increases, you'll soon be able to initiate a conversation with a woman and set up a specific date with her in a matter of minutes before exchanging phone numbers.

The Date of the Reunion

The Planning Stage In the event of a Dump

Your avenues of communication are now open once more. It's crucial that you put more of your attention on getting to know each other again and developing chemistry than you do on a relationship because this will help you both feel at ease around each other for the second time.

It was already established that you shouldn't get in touch with your ex at all if you were dumped. Feel free to ask her out if and when she reaches out to you first. However, you must use extreme caution when doing this. Asking your ex out in a non-threatening, strictly platonic manner is the first step towards setting up a new date. Plan exciting, romantic evening dates instead of "friendship" dates like going out to lunch or coffee. This will allow you to rekindle your chemistry and rekindle your desire. You have to respond if your ex-girlfriend declines to go on a date. 'No worries, if you change your mind, give me a call; I'd love to see you. Or, put it in your own words, "I have to get going, bye." Then, hang up and go about your business. This is quite significant. Act as though you are interested in this woman both romantically and sexually. The simplest way to get injured again is to pretend to be a buddy. Avoid doing this at all costs. Whether or not she is willing to go out, be upfront and honest about the fact that your motives are solely romantic.

If she's not, you just say what you want in a kind and polite way, keep your door open for her, and keep trying to be the greatest version of yourself. You should just cease bringing up the subject of getting together until she does if, despite your repeated attempts to reach out to her, she still won't commit to a specific date. After talking for five minutes or less, hang up the phone and continue the conversation. By your behavior, you are demonstrating to her that you are a self-assured man who knows what he wants and that you will not settle for anything less. If she chooses not to show interest in you back, you will move on until you find someone who will.

The Planning Stage: Should you discard them

Here, the dynamics are a little different. It's only appropriate for you to get in touch with them initially in this situation if you dumped them. Call them, apologize for being a jackass, and explain that you are sorry and would love to see them. Yes, you may have to do a little ass-kissing, but hey, after all, you are the one who kicked them to the curb.

Great if the answer is yes! Arrange a romantic, exciting date; remember, don't focus on the relationship or tying her down; just enjoy yourself. Again, you just reply, "No worries, if you change your mind, give me a call; I'd love to see you" if she says no. I have to go, bye.' You then go on and don't get in touch with her again until she does.

She will answer "YES" without hesitation if there is still a glimmer of romanticism. The secret is to provide her with an offer she can't reject. Being the best version of yourself is that offer.

Six Things to Avoid When Out on a Date

After a long time, you managed to convince her to accept your invitation to a date. You're both anxious and excited, full of hope and yet wary of what can occur. And with good reason—handling this delicately is necessary as it's a vital step in the process of reconciling.

Here are six dos and don'ts to help you make the most of your first date, whether you're going out with your ex-girlfriend tonight, next week, in a few days, or soon:

Don'ts

1. Throughout the discussion, keep the tone humorous. Nobody likes to be in

awkward circumstances. And if you haven't seen your ex in a while, this meeting is probably going to be uncomfortable and unpleasant. However, you can still make things better by being light-hearted. Crack some jokes and make her grin. Make the most of this interaction, and more will undoubtedly come.

2. Keep your excitement in check. After being separated for a while, it's normal to be giddy with anticipation. Just control your exuberance, though. Giving her the idea that you've been looking forward to this meeting is the last thing you want to do. Show her how delighted you are to be with her, but don't go overboard. Guys occasionally fail to

recognize that women could feel a little uneasy if males become overly thrilled to see them. You say it's weird? It's exclusive to girls.

3. Limit the length of the meeting: If all goes as planned, you will find yourself deeply engaged in stimulating discussions. But don't make the mistake of extending your date past the point where you run out of topics to discuss, and she tells you it's time to leave. Continue the momentum until the discussion reaches its zenith, at which point the exchange ends. If she decides to go on a second date, you want to leave her with something to look forward to.

Is It Valuable To Save?

Is it worth the time and energy to try to win your ex back, though? It all relies on your goals for this new or rekindled relationship and whether your ex-partner was content with their life before splitting up with you. Repairing the previous connection can be something worth investigating together if there's a chance that things will turn out better than they were previously.

Consider your goals for the partnership first. Do you both firmly believe that this may develop into a more serious commitment, or are you just looking to get your ex back and resume your friendship? Next, figure out how much effort and time each party will need to put in to improve the situation from the start. Trying it again might not be such a horrible idea after all if there's a good probability of success with little work on either side (not including therapy).

However, this clearly indicates that there are issues that need to be resolved before taking any action to patch things up if one spouse has drastically changed their life since the breakup (e.g., moving away, getting engaged, or getting married) without first talking to the other. Both partners must be committed to the relationship and ready to adjust their lifestyles in order for it to succeed. Refrain from contacting your spouse until further notice if you believe they are not as committed as they should be (for example, they are still abusing drugs or alcohol).

Forcing someone to accept assistance—even if it involves going up against family members—won't help the person who doesn't want it! There are plenty of fish out there waiting for someone just like you; by carrying on this unhealthy cycle of ignoring one another's needs, you're only harming yourself.

It is essential that you both take the time to seriously consider whether this is something worth pursuing in order to win your ex back. Solving these issues together can be a great approach to rekindling the deep affection between two individuals if there are external causes (like a communication breakdown) that keep either person from feeling content and happy in their current circumstances.

However, if everything was going well previously but has since altered as a result of some unanticipated events (such as death), then splitting up might be the wisest course of action at this time. Once more, no matter how much it aches to be apart, you should only give up on someone if they are unwilling or unable to return the favor!

Breakups can occur for a variety of reasons and are not necessarily followed by happily ever after. But you can go so far together if you have the correct amount of love, tolerance, trust, and communication on both ends!

Getting Started Again

After getting dumped, it can be challenging enough to deal with rejection. However, the hurt will probably be more intense if your relationship ends suddenly after several years of dating but continues for a long time. Those who have made significant emotional investments in their relationships are, after all, more likely to be offended by abrupt, seemingly unjustified breakups.

This is the reason why so many ex-partners go through phases where they try to "get over it" without going too far, like getting in touch with their ex or devising complex schemes to win them back (at least not immediately). The issue here is that you can't be sure the other person will take any action to facilitate your situation.

How, then, may this be changed?

The first step is easy: even though it could be a little frightening or terrifying at first, start showing your ex what they could be missing out on if they don't take steps to get back together. This will make them want you again.

Why would someone who had just ended a relationship abruptly turn around after receiving a single text message or phone call from that partner? It may seem unachievable, but keep in mind that most individuals aren't accustomed to rejection and are more likely to flee than to stay put, particularly if there is a better opportunity waiting somewhere else.

You need to make your ex want something they will never have if they don't take action, if you want them to be interested in speaking with you again, or, at the absolute least, in giving your relationship another shot.

Put your creative thinking cap on and come up with some ways to attract your ex's attention without coming across as desperate (or too forward) if this is something that interests you and they haven't gotten back to you after these initial steps.

Here are some suggestions:

Deliver flowers and include a note expressing your sorrow for them.

As soon as you can, invite them over for dinner and chat.

Compose a piece about all the drawbacks of single life and send it to him in an anonymous email so he can see why he is missing out.

To let them know how much time has gone since you last saw them, compile a list of everything you miss about them and send it to their email address in an anonymous manner.

Recall that this is a love letter! Thus, be dedicated to ensuring that, in the unlikely event that he or she decides to reconcile after reading just one letter (or viewing just one text message) from you, this would be the ideal moment to follow through.

The worst thing someone can do, even if it seems pointless, is give up too soon when attempting to get an ex back. On the contrary, it requires more bravery than ever to keep proving to an ex that you value them.

Abolish the Question, "How Can I Make More Friends?"

How do I get more friends? Many people ask this question on a regular basis. Creating new friends won't always happen on your own. Friendships typically develop as a result of repeatedly seeing the same people. We find out through our conversation that we have certain interests in common. Gradually, as we share interests, we gradually expose more and more aspects of ourselves. In the end, we begin to perform a variety of effects together and continue to spend time together just having fun.

Those who struggle with conversation and social awkwardness often find it challenging to form new friendships. Additionally, having low self-esteem makes it difficult to form new friendships. When you do not believe that you're a pleasant, precious person, also you won't be able to believe that other people like you. If you believe that you are disliked by others, you will also not take the time or effort to establish friends.

Still, if you haven't been making as many friends as you would want, the first thing you should do is ask yourself why that has occurred. You won't be able to take appropriate action to improve your circumstances until you recognize what it is that you have been doing or permitting to prevent you from developing friendships.

Here are some things to consider: ask yourself if you want to know what you should be doing differently in your life in order to meet new people.

Do you find it difficult to greet strangers with a smile and a hello? Or do you shy away from conversing with strangers?

Do you frequent groups where you might run into folks who share your interest in certain effects?

Do you think of yourself as a likable, morally upright person?

..Do you think of other individuals as essentially interesting and morally upright mortal beings? Or do you typically view strangers with suspicion?

Do you take the time to find out what other people think and hunt for topics of conversation you both enjoy?

Are you willing to show others that you genuinely care about them by asking them about their thoughts and making non-obtrusive, polite gestures?

..Do you typically have very positive interactions with other people, or do you frequently have negative interactions?

If you want to befriend more people in the future, you should be asking yourself these kinds of questions. If you see that you haven't been truly gregarious, you must also make the necessary changes. It doesn't have to be difficult to learn how to create new acquaintances. Individuals who enjoy spending time and having conversations with one another will be more likely to become friends. Having friendships does not need you to be a glamorous, wealthy, or successful individual. Asking, "How can I be a friend to further people?" is a better question to ask than "How can I make further friends?"

Tips For Befriending Girls?

Furthermore, a lot of males struggle to approach girls when the chance presents itself because they are too bashful or lack confidence in their ability to do so. In fact, some individuals believe that "picking up girls" is morally reprehensible.

Regardless of your rank, your mentality is what keeps you stuck and prevents you from successfully approaching women. Instead of thinking of it as approving of picking up girls, why not think of it as creating new friends? Yes, becoming friends with girls. Does that make more sense now? Only semantics, really. So what really is so restricting or unintentionally incorrect about approaching ladies to be friends? You'll feel more comfortable approaching ladies and striking up conversations with them if you adopt this new perspective.

Almost any man may learn the art of picking up girls unless, of course, he isn't interested in girls. Picking up ladies or rather being friends with them isn't irritating to women at all. The majority of attached women were chosen by their partners and are content with this.

Now, let's look at how to approach girls. Make up your mind to think like a pickup artist before you begin. Imagine yourself as a successful guy who can make friends with women. Pay attention to one thing and one thing only: you're going out to pick up chicks; thus, you should disregard what other women think of you.

You can move on from rejection with ease if you train your mind to focus on this specific goal. Consider each rejection as a step closer to success because, if you stick with it, you will eventually be accepted for who you are. Who knows, maybe your first try will work this time, and if not, whatever, maybe it will work out in the future. But if you don't really try, you won't succeed. Picking up girls may be enjoyable, so try to enjoy yourself when approaching and picking up women. Recall that your only goal is to become friends with women. Therefore, you shouldn't worry about what they think of your strategy or how they understand it. This is due to the fact that the more you stress over these unfounded worries, the lower your confidence will be, which will force you to make clumsy mistakes throughout your girlfriend's attempts.

You have to have something to talk about in mind before you even start to approach a woman. You ought to be prepared for the conversation, know how to tease and flirt with her and know how to enjoy yourself. That is, you need to be prepared with a thoroughly thought-out war strategy.

After making eye contact with your target, you'll feel more secure in your approach when you have a plan in place. Recall that women are drawn to self-assured men, so when you approach a female with a well-prepared essay, you'll come across as more confident and succeed far more with her since you won't make the same mistakes as men who approach women without a plan.

Therefore, picking up girls is simple because most girls are already waiting to be picked up. What makes you believe that you cannot succeed as a pickup artist when you are self-assured and have a solid plan in place? That way, you'll make lots of new friends who are ladies. Is it really not that bad?

Here are a few tactics to help you win the want game:

Put down your eyes.

This will give you both some distance and time to think back on your relationship. You have to respect your ex's decision if they desire space.

Take care of yourself.

Now is a great time to focus on developing yourself, whether that be through personal development or simply taking better care of yourself. When you are at your best, it will be easier to get your ex to want you again.

Manifest your continuous interest in your ex. It's vital to convey to your ex that you are still thinking about them and the connection.

You might achieve this by doing small things, like giving them a thoughtful gift or message.

Remain composed.

It's important to be patient and allow things to unfold gradually. Steer clear of pushing things or hurrying the process.

It's important to show your ex that you've moved on from the issues that led to the breakup of your relationship, if there were any.

This may mean apologizing for past transgressions and demonstrating your want to repair the relationship.

Show consideration for your former partner and avoid making light of them in public by saying nothing positive about them. This will just cause the tension to increase between the two of you.

You should be ready for the potential that things will not work out in your relationship with your ex. You may be trying to get them back, but you need to be prepared in case it doesn't.

Seek assistance

It's normal to feel angry and confused after a breakup. It could be helpful to discuss your feelings with a trusted friend or family member or seek support from a therapist.

When you're playing the wanted game, always have patience and focus on getting your ex to want you again. While you pay attention to and honor your ex's feelings, concentrate on becoming the best version of yourself.

It's important to keep in mind that trying to get your ex back through the wanted game is only one tactic you might employ.

It's not the only choice, and not everybody will be successful using it. If you feel like you've tried everything and the want game isn't working for you, it might be time to consider your options.

As an alternative to the "want game," you can play the "get game," which involves trying to win your ex back via whatever means necessary. You can employ coercion, deception, or other strategies. On the other hand, these tactics usually cause more harm than good in the long run.

If you're considering trying the get game, it's important to decide if it's the right move for you. Is it worth sacrificing your morals and dignity in an attempt to get your ex back? Is it worth it to take a chance on the possible harm these tactics can cause to your relationship and ex?

Ultimately, the best approach is to be sincere, polite, and willing to consider the possibility that things might not work out while attempting to get your ex back.

Your top priority should be to be the greatest version of yourself and show your ex that you are still engaged in them and the relationship.

This could include staying away from touch, becoming better, and showing your former partner how far you've come.

It's important to remember that engaging in the wanted game necessitates understanding and respecting your ex's feelings.

Don't try to convince or compel your ex to want you again. Instead, show your ex that you are still engaged in them and the relationship by being the greatest version of yourself.

It's no secret that men love to chase after things they think they can't have.

Sadly, a lot of women take things too far and choose to date someone else only to attract their former partner's attention. This never works.

If you go straight to another guy, you'll be telling him that your relationship wasn't meaningful to you and that you've already moved on.

He's not going to do something about it, even if he does still feel something for you.

All it takes to play hard to get is to remember not to drop what you're doing and hurry to him/her the moment they call. When you're feeling really happy, give them a callback and let the call go to voice mail.

You can accept their recommendation for a date if you change the suggested day. He or she might be interested in getting together for coffee on Fridays, for example.

Decide to meet for coffee, but inform them that Friday will be hectic and that Saturday would be a better time for you.

It doesn't matter what else you decide to do on the recommended day; you can call a friend, watch a movie, or give your dog a bath. Just make sure they know about your own obligations.

If they want to take part again, they will need to work hard to catch your attention.

Plan ahead for a follow-up meeting so that when you do ultimately run into them again, you will be under pressure to keep to a time restriction. Tell them you have to leave at a certain time since you can't stay long.

This usually means cutting your conversation short if you've been enjoying each other's company; otherwise, he or she will be left wanting more.

Avoid the temptation to call them right after your initial meeting to arrange another date. Watch to see whether they contact you after a few days.

Keep in mind that the causes behind your breakup are still very much present in their mind. After just one meeting with you in your former persona, they won't be able to let go of the problems that led to your estrangement.

You will need to make an effort to rekindle those sentiments if you truly want them back.

But think carefully about your play-hard-to-get tactics. You do not want to become one of those people who are hard to want, do you? These are the ones who cross the line from arrogance to confidence.

Even when doing so causes friction, they are not afraid to voice their strong opinions. They insist that they had nothing to do with the breakup of the relationship and blame their ex solely for it.

If, while out on a date with your ex, your thoughts start to turn sour, be ready to call it quits and head home while things are still going well. If you don't, you could end up losing them forever.

Contents Table of

Overview

Chapter 1: Your Primary Goals

Chapter 2: Prospects for Resuming the Connection

Chapter 3: Making Positive Changes in Yourself

Chapter 4: Make Up with Your Past

Chapter 5: Moving Slowly

Chapter 6: Have Honesty

Chapter 7: The Influence of Memories

Chapter 8: A Sedate Approach

Chapter 9: The Second Time Around, Love Is More Beautiful

In summary

Reunite with your ex

The Step-by-Step Manual for Quickly Getting Your Ex Back

© Fred Redding 2015 Copyright - All rights reserved.

The purpose of this document is to give accurate and trustworthy information on the subject and problem discussed. The publication is marketed under the false impression that the publisher is exempt from providing officially authorized, qualified, or accounting services. A qualified practitioner should be consulted if legal or professional counsel is required.

- From a Declaration of Principles that both a Committee of Publishers and Associations and an American Bar Association Committee recognized and approved in equal measure.

No portion of this text may be copied, reproduced, or transmitted in any form or by any electronic or hard copy means. It is highly forbidden to record this publication, and storing it longer than necessary without the publisher's explicit consent is also illegal. All rights reserved.

The material presented here is claimed to be accurate and consistent, with the caveat that the receiving reader bears sole and complete responsibility for any liability resulting from misuse or inattention while using any of the policies, procedures, or instructions included. The publisher shall not be subject to any legal liability or blame for any damages, compensation, or financial loss resulting from the information contained in this publication, whether caused directly or indirectly.

All copyrights not owned by the publisher belong to their respective authors.

This information is general in nature and is provided only for informational reasons. The information is being presented without any kind of warranty or obligation.

The trademarks are used without authorization, and the trademark owners have neither supported nor granted permission for the trademark to be published. The brands and trademarks used in this book are held by their respective owners and are merely used for clarification; they are not associated with this work.

Introduction

Thank you for downloading Get Your Ex Back: The Step-by-Step Guide on How to Get Your Ex Back Fast! I also want to congratulate you on your success.

This book offers tried-and-true methods for rekindling your romance and persuading your ex to give you another go.

It's never easy to break up with someone, especially if you still feel something for them. Occasionally, you come to the realization that the reasons for your breakup were not healthy, and as a result, you start to long to attempt your relationship again.

You can use the questions in Chapter 1 to determine whether you are truly interested in getting your ex back or whether you are merely itching or searching for a one-night companion. Chapter 2 provides a list of signs to help you assess the likelihood of a reconciliation with your ex after assisting you in deciding if this is truly something you want to do. Chapter 3 offers advice on how to better yourself, as this will demonstrate to your former partner that you are not just a "stranger." Practical advice for reintegrating into your ex's life gradually and without pressuring them to make snap judgments about the future of your relationship may be found in Chapters 4 through 8. Chapter 9 wraps up your project and provides insightful guidance on what to do if your ex rejects or accepts your advances.

I appreciate you downloading this book once more, and I hope you enjoy it!

Chapter 1: Your Primary Goals

Prior to devising any plans on how to win your ex back, ask yourself the following questions: Are you truly interested in reuniting? Why?

Seeking a one-night partner when feeling lonely is one thing. Another is actually missing someone and wanting to spend time with them again—not simply for a booty call. Make sure you have the correct motivations before taking any action to get your ex back.

You can use the following self-assessment questions to decide whether you're merely itching or if you're fully devoted to this project:

Do you believe the grounds for your breakup weren't right?

Does it truly merit a second try?

This time, are you prepared to give in?

When you're with him or her, are you authentic?

Are you prepared to give your relationship more time to succeed?

Are you prepared to talk about your previous problems and work toward a solution?

Have you changed for the better since the split?

Has your exchange changed for the better after you split up?

Will your decision to win your ex back be supported by your friends and family?

Do you imagine yourself spending a long time together with this person?

Will you be at your best around this person?

Well, it would be excellent if you answered "yes" to the majority of these questions. However, if the majority of your responses are negative, you might want to put off your plans, give it some thought, and consider whether you truly want to be in a relationship with this person once more. You don't want to spend time and energy trying to reignite your relationship just to realize afterward that you still feel the same way you always did and that you weren't meant to be together.

Chapter 2: Prospects for Resuming the Connection

It's one thing to want your ex back; it's quite another to truly win them back. Sometimes, you're trapped on the first one, no matter how much you desire for the second one to happen.

Here are a few signs to assist you in determining whether you should pursue a prior romantic interest again:

How long the relationship has been going

In general, it's simpler to repair a three-year relationship than a short-lived romance that ended after two months. The likelihood of getting your ex back increases with the length of time you have been together. This is because your time together has allowed you to forge bonds that are difficult to sever.

The degree of commitment in the partnership

It is simpler to sort things up in the event that you have a falling out if you have reached the stage in your relationship where you have discussed marriage intentions or, at the very least, have presented each other to your respective families and friends. Living together or investing in something together in the past can also serve as a barometer for the seriousness of your relationship and the likelihood that you will reconcile.

The cause of your split

Whether or not you can win your ex back depends in large part on the cause of your breakup. Some couples end their relationship for the most trivial reasons: a bad date gone wrong, one partner forgetting their anniversary or another significant date, or a disagreement over a point of contention. While these may appear petty, they are the true causes of hundreds of breakups in the past. The good news is that it's simpler to resolve this kind of split. Sometimes, despite these misunderstandings, all a couple needs is some time apart to realize they still love each other and want to be together. Nevertheless, it is more difficult to resolve problems with physical closeness (long-distance relationships), incompatibility, and conflicts in future aspirations and ambitions.

The manner in which you terminated your partnership

When you and your lover decide that you are happier apart than together, it's a good breakup. You decide to stay in touch with each other and part ways as friends. Since the ex-lovers separated amicably and both of them know they want the best for the other, amicable breakups like these are easier to repair. Additionally, you have more opportunities to think back on the good moments you shared in the past if you and your ex are still in close contact. This could eventually make you want to give them another chance. On the other hand, since you and your ex have not ended things amicably, a terrible breakup characterized by a lot of yelling, accusations, and crying is more difficult to resolve.

The adjustments you've made since the split

The reason you and your ex are trying again is that you both feel that you work better together and that you can resolve issues that have come up in the past. This will mostly rely on the adjustments you have made to your life since parting ways. Have you made the effort to learn more about who you are? Have you developed personally? Can you now handle disagreements better? Reuniting doesn't really make sense if your ex and you haven't adjusted your attitudes toward each other following your breakup; you'll eventually break up again.

These are only indicators, after all, so don't get too depressed if the majority of them don't go in your favor. In the end, you still have to figure out how to get your ex back, and the next few chapters will walk you through the process.

www.ingramcontent.com/pod-product-compliance
Lightning Source LLC
Chambersburg PA
CBHW052143110526
44591CB00012B/1834